*The Dragon of Thistleberry
and other stories*

# The Dragon of Thistleberry and other stories

*Barbara Wilton*

Illustrated by Jon Miller

HODDER AND STOUGHTON

LONDON   SYDNEY   AUCKLAND   TORONTO

British Library Cataloguing in Publication Data

Wilton, Barbara
 The dragon of Thistleberry and other stories.
 I. Title    II. Miller, Jon. *1947–*
 823'.914[J]    PZ7

 ISBN 0-340-38734-3

Published by Hodder and Stoughton Children's Books,
a division of Hodder and Stoughton Ltd,
Mill Road, Dunton Green, Sevenoaks, Kent TN13 2YJ

Photoset by Rowland Phototypesetting Ltd,
Bury St Edmunds, Suffolk

Printed in Great Britain by St Edmundsbury Press,
Bury St Edmunds, Suffolk.

# Contents

# The Dragon of Thistleberry

Thistleberry is not all that far away but it's not very easy to get to. You can't go in your car or get on a bus, because no roads go there.

Once you could go by train, and that was lovely. A bright red engine pulled three yellow railway carriages, and puffed out clouds of soft blue smoke. When you looked out of the carriage windows, you could see peppermint fields, candy cows and tiny villages where smiling people lived in chocolate cake houses. But that was a long time ago.

Then something happened in Thistleberry, and everyone stopped going there. So the bright red engine had to stay in its shed. Grass and weeds grew over the railway track until it was quite hidden, and everyone forgot where it was.

There is still just one way you can get to

Thistleberry, but it's a secret, at least for the moment.

So who lives in Thistleberry, and why don't people want to go there any more?

Well, it's a magic town, and, as you know, only magic people can live in magic towns. If un-magic people stayed there, they wouldn't know the spells which make everything work.

So everyone in Thistleberry is either a fairy or a wizard. There are one or two witches who have had the nasty taken out of their spells, and even a few of the better-behaved goblins. And they all love music.

Everyone can play something and they used to practise all day. So whenever you went by a house, you could hear either a piano, or a violin, or a trombone, or even a bluebell or a foxglove. Because, of course, when a magic person blows into the tiny trumpet of a bluebell or a foxglove, the most lovely sound comes out.

Amelia was a fairy, and she lived alone in a small house in Thistleberry. She liked being on her own as she was rather shy and a bit scared of talking to people. She made magic fairy cakes that could change into any colour you wished. She also played beautiful tunes on a tiny whistle;

but she played very quietly so no one would notice her. Just how well she played is very important, as you will see later.

One day a dragon moved into a cave in the hill just behind the town. He was huge with red scales on his back.

It was a Monday, which was market day. Everyone in the town had a little shop or a table where they piled all the fruit and vegetables they had grown in their gardens, for people to buy. Amelia was there too. She had a table in a quiet corner where she sold her magic cakes.

Everyone was talking about the dragon, but very few of them had actually seen him. Amelia was too shy to say anything, but she listened carefully.

All at once the sky went very dark, and the dragon could be seen flying towards the market place. As he flapped his great green wings, he made such a wind that everybody's washing blew down and got dirty. They were very cross but were much too afraid to say anything about it. Amelia was more afraid than anyone else. She hid under her table of magic cakes and hoped she wouldn't be seen.

The dragon landed right in the middle of

everything. He knocked over all the tables, sending tomatoes, apples and oranges bouncing all over the place.

The people of Thistleberry were very surprised and frightened. Some tried to run away, but they slipped on the fruit and couldn't get up again. Others just stood and stared. Then the dragon gave a great puff. Orange flames came out of his mouth, turning a pile of red tomatoes quite black in just a second. No one had ever seen anything like it. Amelia sat under her table, shaking with fright.

Then, in a louder, puffier, smokier voice than you've ever heard, the dragon spoke. As he did so, his breath showed in white clouds of steam.

'LISTEN TO ME, ALL OF YOU!'

The people listened. Well, you would, wouldn't you?

'I CAME HERE FOR SOME PEACE AND QUIET, AND I'M NOT GETTING ANY. YOUR NOISE . . .'

He meant their music, but to him it was just a noise.

'. . . YOUR NOISE GOES ON ALL DAY, JUST WHEN I'M TRYING TO SLEEP!'

You see, dragons like to sleep when we're awake, and are awake when we're asleep.

'THIS HAS GOT TO STOP,' said the dragon. 'THERE MUST BE NO MORE NOISE!'

He gave an extra big puff and blew a bit of fire. This was to make sure everyone knew that he really meant what he said.

'IF I HEAR ONE MORE BIT OF NOISE, I SHALL COME BACK ON A MONDAY AND EAT THREE OF YOU. THEN I'LL EAT ANOTHER THREE!'

Of course he could have said he would eat six of them, but dragons are not very good at adding up. This dragon did not know any numbers bigger than three.

Of course everyone was very very frightened. Amelia was still under her table. She had never been so scared.

The dragon huffed and puffed again, and said in a voice like thunder:

'DO YOU ALL PROMISE NOT TO MAKE ANY MORE NOISE?'

They all nodded their heads. One or two people said 'Yes', but very quietly. They didn't dare make a noise.

'RIGHT!' said the dragon. 'NOW I'M GOING BACK TO BED!'

He flapped his wings so hard that some people had their hats blown away. Then the dragon flew over their heads and went back to his cave.

The people of Thistleberry were very sad. Without music, their town would be such an unhappy place. And no one likes to visit an unhappy place. But with a dragon as horrid as that, what could they do?

Amelia came out from under her table. Without saying anything to anyone, she went home. She was thinking very hard.

As time went by, Thistleberry became sadder

and sadder. The people got very lonely because no one came to visit them. Of course they dared not play any music, not even a tiny blow on a bluebell. The dragon might hear even the smallest sound and they were so scared in case he came back.

All the pianos, the violins and the trombones became covered in dust. No one picked any foxglove trumpets from their gardens, and no one did any smiling. In fact they did a lot of crying; but very quietly.

In her little house, Amelia didn't do any smiling or crying. But she did do a lot of thinking. Every day, as she baked her magic cakes, she thought and thought. She wanted so much to bring music back to Thistleberry. She even had an idea of how to do it. The trouble was that she would have to be very brave and, as we know, Amelia was not very brave at all.

Then a day came when she couldn't do any more thinking. Amelia made up her mind. She baked an extra big pile of magic fairy cakes and put them in her shopping basket. Then she picked up her tiny whistle.

'I do hope I can remember how to play it,' she said to herself.

Because of course she hadn't been able to play any music for a long time.

She wrapped the whistle in a clean handkerchief and tucked it in her basket next to the magic cakes. She waited until it was nearly dark and went outside. She shut her front door, very quietly, and walked through the town, feeling more frightened than ever before. On the side of the hill behind Thistleberry, she saw a big dark hole. It was the dragon's cave!

Amelia crept up to the opening of the cave. Even fairies don't like going out at night, and she knew she had to go into the cave, where the moonbeams could not reach to light her way.

She waited at the entrance for a moment and tried to make herself feel a bit braver. Then there was a huge rumble which made the hill shake. It was the dragon snoring! He would soon wake up and go hunting for his breakfast. She would have to be quick.

Still holding her basket of magic cakes and the whistle, Amelia walked on through the darkness. Spiders' webs brushed against her face, and once she trod on something squishy. Whatever it was, it gave a loud squeak and she heard its feet patter away in a rush.

Then, in the distance, she saw two red lights. As she walked on, they got nearer and nearer. The dragon's eyes! She knew he had seen her because he called out in an enormous voice.

'OH GOOD! BREAKFAST IN BED!'

Amelia knew he wanted her for his breakfast, and it gave her a very nasty feeling. But she pretended not to know what he meant.

'Yes,' she said in a small voice. 'I've brought you some magic cakes, Oh Great and Wonderful Dragon!'

It was very clever of her to call him 'Great and Wonderful'. Dragons love to be called things like that, and it stops them thinking about breakfast.

'COME HERE,' said the dragon. 'LET ME HAVE A LOOK.'

Poor Amelia! She had to go right up to him! He seemed even bigger than when he had flown into town on that Monday, so long ago. He stared at her through his bright red eyes, and she noticed that his nose was all black from the fire he puffed out.

She held out her basket and the dragon looked inside. He took a magic cake which looked like a tiny bead in his big green claw. He popped it straight into his mouth and swallowed it whole.

'BIT SMALL, ISN'T IT?' he said. 'I'D HARDLY CALL THAT BREAKFAST!'

'Oh, there's lots more in the basket,' said Amelia. 'And if you chew them first, they taste quite nice. And they will turn into any colour you like.'

The dragon looked surprised. He loved colours.

'REALLY?' he said. 'LET ME TRY.'

He picked up another cake, and closed his eyes. He must have made a wish, for the little

brown cake suddenly turned a lovely yellow. The dragon opened his eyes and when he saw the cake, he said,

'GOODNESS ME! IT WORKED! WHAT DO I DO NOW?'

'You eat it, of course,' said Amelia. She was getting a bit braver.

The dragon put the cake into his mouth and chewed it. He tasted the honey and butterdew Amelia always mixed in. She waited, hoping so much that he would enjoy it.

'NOT BAD,' said the dragon, 'NOT AT ALL BAD. GIVE ME ANOTHER!'

Amelia did not yet feel brave enough to remind him that he should have said 'Please'. She gave him the basket and he took the cakes, one by one. Each time he ate one he made a wish, until he had almost run out of colours. Then all the cakes had gone.

'WHAT'S THIS?' he said, and he picked up the only thing left in the basket. It was Amelia's whistle, still wrapped in the handkerchief.

Amelia felt frightened all over again. Would her idea work, or would the dragon get angry and eat her after all?

The dragon dropped the handkerchief on the

floor and looked very hard at the whistle. He had no idea what it was! He was starting to get bored, and Amelia was afraid he might talk about breakfast again.

'It's a whistle,' she said to him. 'Would you like me to play you some music?'

'DOES THAT MEAN YOU'RE GOING TO MAKE A NOISE?' asked the dragon, getting a bit cross.

'Only a tiny noise, and a very nice one,' replied Amelia.

'OH ALL RIGHT!' said the dragon. 'BUT I WON'T LIKE IT, YOU KNOW!'

So Amelia played the quietest, most gentle tune she knew. And believe it or not, the dragon began to close his eyes. The lovely sound was making him sleepy! After a little while she stopped playing.

'I DIDN'T TELL YOU TO STOP,' complained the dragon. 'GO ON! GO ON! PLAY SOME MORE!'

So Amelia played, and the dragon got sleepy again. Soon she began to get tired from all the blowing, but she didn't dare to stop. The dragon's mouth opened in a sort of smile as he slept, and she felt it was safe to stop

playing. He yawned and opened his eyes.

'IS THAT MUSIC?' he asked.

Amelia said that it was. She felt brave enough to tell him how everyone in Thistleberry loved it. She explained how they had stopped playing because they were frightened of him, but how sad and lonely they all were.

The dragon said that was all very well, but when everyone played their music at once, it kept him awake. So Amelia told him her idea.

If the dragon would try sleeping at night and being awake in the daytime, like everyone else, the people of Thistleberry could play their music without bothering him.

'AND WHEN DO I GO HUNTING FOR MY FOOD?' asked the dragon. 'THE THINGS I LIKE TO EAT, SUCH AS BATS, OWLS AND BAD WITCHES, ONLY COME OUT AT NIGHT!'

'But you liked my magic cakes, didn't you?' said Amelia.

'WELL, YES, I SUPPOSE I DID,' the dragon agreed huffily.

'Well then,' said Amelia, 'I'll bring you some cakes every day, then you won't have to go out at night.'

The dragon went very quiet. He was thinking things over.

Amelia had another idea.

'If you like,' she offered, 'I'll even come and play to you each night to send you off to sleep.'

That made the dragon very pleased.

'YES' he said, 'YOU MUST DO THAT!'

Then Amelia said a very brave thing.

'Only if you say "please",' she told him.

The dragon huffed and puffed and said, 'OH, ALL RIGHT THEN. "PLEASE."'

And so it was all settled.

Imagine the delight of everyone in Thistleberry when they heard the good news. They could play their music again, all day long if they wanted to!

Of course they all thought Amelia was wonderfully brave. The Mayor made a speech in her honour in the market place the very next Monday. Everyone stood up and shouted 'Three Cheers!' They wanted Amelia to make a speech, but when they looked round, she was nowhere to be seen. Guess where she was! She'd hidden under her table of magic cakes because she couldn't bear to have all the people looking at her!

So everything turned out well. Amelia did just as she had promised. She baked magic cakes every day and took them to the dragon. Every night she played for him on her whistle until he went to sleep.

The people of Thistleberry are hoping to have visitors again, now that their town is a happy place once more. There is even talk of finding the railway track so the train can go there, but that hasn't happened yet.

Until it does, there's still only the secret way to get to Thistleberry. I'll tell *you* what it is, if you promise not to tell anyone else. First, you must eat a magic cake for your tea. (Don't forget to mix in some honey and butterdew!) If the cake turns into a colour when you make a wish, it means the magic will work, and that night, in your dreams, you can fly to Thistleberry. But fly quietly – after all, you don't want to wake the dragon!

# Amelia and the Lost Mermaid

Amelia loved the river. On a sunny morning she would often wander along its bank. Sometimes she found a nice flat stone to sit on, and would dangle her toes in the cool sparkling water. The river was so clear that you could see lovely coloured stones right at the bottom. Amelia would stay there a long time, thinking about nothing in particular, which is just the thing to do in a peaceful place.

One morning, as she walked along the river path, she heard loud voices.

'Bother!' she thought. 'It's the river pixies. It won't be very peaceful with them around.'

Sure enough, round a gentle bend in the river, there they were. Amelia counted ten of them. Each had a shiny pink face and wore a neat suit with a belt of woven grass. They were fishing, and making a lot of noise as they called to one another. Although river pixies never seem to stop talking and teasing, they are not much bigger than fairies and are quite harmless, so Amelia was not afraid of them.

When they caught sight of her, they shouted even more.

'I can see a fairy! I can see a fairy!'

Amelia wished they would go away so she could have the river bank to herself, but she said politely:

'Good morning! Have you caught any fish yet?'

'Not a thing!' answered a pixie called Bert. He was the only one fishing with a net. All the others were using fishing rods.

'You won't ever catch anything in that stupid net, Bert!' teased another pixie. 'I don't know why you don't use a proper rod like everyone else!'

'I should have thought,' said Amelia, 'that none of you will catch anything if you make so much noise. You must have frightened all the fish away!'

'Oh, listen to her!' they all shouted. 'Little Miss Cleverclogs! What does a fairy know about fishing?'

Amelia didn't know anything about fishing, but she was about to tell them it was just a matter of common sense, when Bert gave a great yell. The stick to which his net was fixed had begun to bend. He had caught something!

All the pixies gathered round and helped Bert lift the net from the river. Up it came, dripping and sparkling in the sun. They laid it on the grass and peered inside.

'What have you got, Bert? What have you got?' shouted a small pixie at the back who was too short to see over their shoulders.

'I can't see it myself yet,' said Bert. 'Now be quiet, Arnold, or I'll throw you in the river!'

Little Arnold kept quiet, but he jumped up and down trying to see inside the net. Amelia came closer, because she wanted to have a look as well.

The net was now flat on the ground. A tiny creature sat huddled inside. It looked rather like a fairy, but at the same time not at all like a fairy. It looked a bit like a fish, but not exactly like a fish.

'Funny sort of fairy!' said Bert. 'It hasn't any legs.'

They all stared. Sure enough, it had no legs.

Maurice, a slow thoughtful pixie, gave the

tiny creature a long look.

'Even more of a funny fairy, Bert,' he said. 'It's got a tail, just like a fish. What do you make of that?'

'Seems a bit fishy to me!' answered Bert, and they all laughed.

'Let me see! Please let me have a look!' pleaded Arnold, who still hadn't seen anything.

The pixies moved out of the way and Arnold elbowed his way to front of the group. Amelia slipped through as well, and they gazed at the fish-fairy.

'Well, Miss Cleverclogs Fairy!' said Bert, 'you reckon to know so much about things. What is it?' He nudged his friends and winked at them.

Amelia looked at the fairy face and the long, wet strands of hair. She looked at the shiny green scales on the delicate tail. She knew exactly what it was.

'It's a mermaid,' she said quietly.

'A what?' demanded Bert.

'A mermaid,' repeated Amelia. 'Half fairy, half fish; she must have come all the way from the sea.'

The river pixies for once said nothing. They'd

never heard of a mermaid, let alone seen one.
Amelia must be clever after all.

'I wonder how she came to be in the Thistleberry river,' said Amelia.

'Why don't you ask her?' suggested Arnold.
'Go on, I dare you, ask her!'

Arnold didn't often have sensible ideas, but
this was one of them.

'Hallo!' said Amelia to the mermaid. 'What's
your name?'

The mermaid looked up and brushed the wet
hair from her face. Her cheeks were wet and
Amelia wasn't sure if it was river water or if she
was crying.

'I'm Eleanor,' whispered the mermaid.
'Eleanor Ferny Frond, and I'm lost. Please help
me!'

'Of course we'll help you,' said Amelia. 'How
did you become lost?'

'I was swimming with my family near my
home in the sea,' explained Eleanor, 'I just swam
in to explore this beautiful cave, and when I came
out again, all my family had disappeared.'

The pixies all said 'Oh dear!' because they
were really rather soft-hearted.

'I swam and swam, looking for them,' said

25

Eleanor, beginning to cry, 'I must have come all the way up this river, and now I'm lost!'

'Don't worry,' said Amelia, 'we'll help you find your way home.'

She took charge of things, and the pixies seemed not to mind being told what to do. Amelia was clever and that meant she'd be good at making plans.

'Now, has anyone got a big shell?' she asked.

'I have,' said Bert. 'It's been on my mantelpiece for ages. What do you want it for?'

Amelia explained that mermaids can't live in houses. They can only come out of the water for a short time, or they die. If they put the big shell in the water, Eleanor Ferny Frond could spend the night in it.

So Bert fetched the shell and they put it in the water, just deep enough so that it was covered. All the pixies helped, especially Arnold, who had taken rather a liking to the little mermaid.

'What did you say your name was?' he asked her.

When she told him 'Eleanor Ferny Frond' he said: 'That's too long a name for me to remember. Is it all right if I just call you "Effie"?'

So 'Effie' she was, from that moment.

In the evening, when Effie was asleep in her shell, Amelia and the pixies had a meeting.

'Right!' said Amelia, 'Effie is safe and happy for the moment, but we must help her back to the sea.'

'How shall we do that?' asked Bert.

'We'll take a boat and guide her back,' she replied.

'I want to come!' shouted Arnold. 'Please let me come!'

'What on earth for?' asked Bert.

'Because she likes me, Effie does!' said Arnold, going red in the face.

'Because you like her, you mean!' teased Bert. 'What a silly soft pudding you are, Arnold!'

So it was all arranged. Bert would borrow his uncle's boat the next day, and he, Maurice, Amelia and Arnold would take Effie back to the sea. Amelia had never been on such an adventure before, and she hoped to herself that it would be all right.

The next morning they were up early. Bert fetched the boat while Maurice and Arnold made a little rope harness to fit under Effie's arms. A rope would be fixed to the harness and Arnold, in the boat, would hold the rope. In this way they could all keep together and if Effie got tired of swimming, the rope would pull her along.

At last they were all set and the other pixies came to wave them off. Amelia sat at the back of the boat with Arnold and the rope which was fixed to Effie in the water. Bert and Arnold were to do the rowing. As they moved away from the bank and the waving pixies, Bert had a sudden thought.

'Hey!' he shouted. 'We haven't got any food!'

'Oh stop worrying, Bert!' said Amelia, 'I've brought some buns, cakes, fruit and some cowslip wine. We've got all we need.'

'Trust you to think of everything, Miss Cleverclogs!' said Bert, but he was really very grateful.

On and on the pixies rowed. Arnold kept an eye on Effie to make sure she wasn't being pulled

too fast. Amelia enjoyed every minute of the journey. It was so peaceful, just watching the world slip by. Once or twice they asked a passing fish how far it was to the sea. There was still a long way to go.

They stopped for lunch on the river bank so that Bert and Maurice could rest their aching arms. Rowing is very hard work and their hands were getting sore. Effie sat in the shallow water and Amelia had a paddle. But they couldn't stop for long and were soon on their way once more.

Towards evening they began to look for a place to stop for the night. The river was no longer clear and bright. It flowed very slowly and Effie told them she could feel lots of nasty weeds flapping round her. Bert and Maurice were so tired they could hardly row. Then there

was a scrunching noise and the boat stopped completely in the middle of the river.

'What's happened?' asked Amelia. 'Why have we stopped?'

'Trouble!' said Maurice gloomily, 'I reckon we've run aground.'

'I think you're right, Maurice,' said Bert, his voice slow and weary. 'That noise was the boat scraping on a rock or something. Sorry, everyone, but we're just plain stuck!'

They were all thinking how horrid it would be to spend the night on the river, when Arnold had another sensible idea.

He took off his shoes, clambered over the side of the boat and went round the back to give it a good push.

'Ugh!' he cried and shuddered as his toes squelched through mud and weeds. He told Effie to keep well out of the way, put his shoulder to the boat, and pushed with all his might. Nothing happened.

'Looks as if you need the muscle mob!' called Maurice, and he was soon round with Arnold. 'Come on, Arnold, put your back into it!' he shouted.

The two pixies pushed and shoved and pushed

again. Still the boat would not move. Poor Effie was getting cold and it was almost dark.

'One last try!' called Amelia. 'On the count of three . . . One . . . two . . . THREE!'

A huge push, and suddenly the boat shot forward. Maurice and Arnold fell flat on their faces in the river! They were soaked through, of course, but had a good laugh about it.

They steered the boat to the bank. The wet pixies had no dry clothes so they spent a very uncomfortable night rolled up in the grass. But at least the boat was safe.

In the morning they were stiff with cold. After eating a bun each, they set off once more. It was a bright, windy day and their damp clothes soon dried. Effie had a word with a bad-tempered river snake as he wriggled by.

'It's not much further now!' she called to the others. 'We'll soon be at the sea!'

Amelia dipped her hand in the water and licked her wet fingers.

'It's salty!' she cried. 'That means it's sea water!'

Their cold night was forgotten. They were going to make it!

'There's a bend ahead,' said Bert. 'Once we're

round that, I bet we'll be at the sea!'

Effie laughed happily. Nearly home!

As they rowed round the river bend the water became white and frothy. The boat started to rock from side to side.

'It's waves!' shouted Arnold. 'Real sea waves!'

'Oh no it isn't,' said Maurice. 'Just have a look at what's coming!'

They looked, and their excitement turned to fear. A whirlpool!

'Can't you row round it?' cried Amelia.

'Not a chance,' replied Bert. 'We're being dragged right into it. All we can do is try to hang on.'

The boat came nearer and nearer to the whirlpool. They could see its dark, angry centre, spinning and gurgling. It was waiting to whizz them round and suck them down!

'Hold tight, Effie!' called Arnold, clinging to the rope.

Then the whirlpool got them. It swung the boat round, slowly at first, then faster and faster. Everything around them turned to a blur and they got very dizzy. Water splashed in over the side of the boat and Amelia wondered what would happen to poor Effie.

Just when they felt they couldn't hang on any longer, the whirlpool threw them clear. They rocked and bobbed through the choppy water until the river carried them to a quieter spot. They gasped for breath and began to empty water from the boat with their cups.

Arnold had somehow managed to hold on to the rope and he pulled it in. But Effie was not on the end. Amelia and the pixies were horrified. They felt sure she must have been sucked down by the whirlpool.

Sadly, Bert and Maurice rowed over towards the bank. Arnold and Amelia sat staring at the water, half hoping Effie might pop up. But she didn't.

Then a bright voice called to them from the water's edge.

'Hallo! Are you all right?'

It was Effie! They were so happy they nearly jumped out of the boat in excitement.

'The rope broke,' Effie told them, 'and I was washed over to the bank.'

'Thank goodness!' said Amelia. 'We thought we'd lost you for ever!'

Arnold just patted Effie's tail and smiled at her. He was too happy to say anything.

'And now,' said Bert, 'it's on to the sea!'

'What do you mean?' asked Effie in surprise. 'Haven't you noticed? We're there!'

Amelia and the pixies had been too busy to look around them. Now they saw that the river had opened up into a wide bay. Beyond that, there was just sea, and more sea. They'd arrived!

'And look!' shouted Effie, 'there's all my family!'

Out in the bay, on a big rock which stuck up out of the water, was a group of mermaids. Effie waved wildly and they began to wave back.

'They've been waiting for me,' she said. 'Now I must go to them.'

She turned to Amelia and the pixies.

'I don't know how to thank you,' she said, 'I'd never have found my way back alone.'

'That's all right, Effie,' said Amelia, 'we've had a lovely adventure. Now don't keep your family waiting. Off you go!'

'Goodbye then,' said Effie, 'Goodbye, all of you, and thank you.'

Amelia, Bert and Maurice said goodbye. Arnold went very red and whispered:

'Go safely, Effie, and goodbye.'

She began to swim away from them, out towards the rock. The waiting mermaids dived into the sea and hurried to meet her. Amelia and the pixies saw her turn and give them a last wave before she dived down and was gone.

For a long time they stared out to sea. Then Bert said:

'Well, it's back to good old Thistleberry for us. Let's get rowing, Maurice!'

Amelia looked at Arnold who was wiping his eyes with a handkerchief.

'What's the matter, Arnold?' she asked.

'Oh, nothing,' said Arnold quickly, 'I must have got sea water in my eyes, but I'm all right now.'

And so they made their way home.

# Mildred's Broomstick

As you know, every witch has a broomstick to fly on. And the bigger and stronger the broomstick, the better the witch's magic power.

Mildred was the smallest witch in Thistleberry. Her broomstick was very thin and spindly, which meant that her magic never worked properly. It also meant that she couldn't fly very far.

Mildred didn't mind that because, believe it or not, she was the only witch in Thistleberry who was afraid of flying. If she went even a tiny bit above the ground she felt quite sick, and just the thought of flying high in the sky made her knees wobble. The other witches were kind and understanding. They never teased her about her fear, but that didn't stop Mildred feeling very left out of things.

Every night all the other witches would race around the stars, shouting in excitement. Poor Mildred would stand by her front door and watch them.

'I do wish I wasn't so afraid!' she would think sadly. 'They're having such fun up there!'

Once or twice, when no one was looking, she'd give it another try. But it was always the same. Her thin broomstick could only manage a few hops, and even that made her feel most uncomfortable. Then Mildred would have to sit down with a cup of brew until she felt better.

'Perhaps I'll have a good strong broomstick one day,' she'd say to herself, 'and then perhaps I'll be braver.'

But she didn't really believe that would ever happen.

One night, as the other witches got ready for their flying, the wind started to blow very hard. It came in huge gusts which tugged at their cloaks and pulled at their hats.

Bubblepot, the Head Witch, settled herself on

her great big broomstick. She could fly safely in any weather but she knew how dangerous a strong wind could be if you weren't careful.

'It's blowing up very rough tonight, girls,' she said to them. 'Keep close together, and no showing off, you younger ones!'

Some of the young witches loved to try out somersaults and have upside-down races, but this was not the sort of night for that!

'Everybody ready?' called Bubblepot, tucking her cloak firmly around her. 'All set for take-off! Up we go!'

And up they went, further and further, until Mildred could just see them as tiny dots dipping and swirling round the stars. They were loving every minute of it, but Mildred got a nasty feeling in her tummy just watching them.

'Oh goodness!' she thought, 'I could never do that, even if I had the strongest broomstick in the world!'

She decided to go to bed and was on her way upstairs, when the wind blew a sudden terrific gust. It came through every tiny crack it could find, rattling the windows and pulling the curtains. She thought for a moment that it might whisk her roof away!

She hurried back to the window. Were the witches all right? No, they weren't! In the moonlight Mildred could see them as they fell through the night sky. Only one of them seemed to be in control.

'That must be Bubblepot,' Mildred said aloud. 'Only she could cope in a gale like this.'

The others were having an awful time, being blown all over the place. One by one they fell towards the ground, their cloaks spread out like wings.

'Oh my word!' gasped the little witch, 'I must go out and help them!'

Grabbing her thick cloak and her little broomstick (because you never know when you might need one), she rushed out into the angry night.

As she got nearer to the village she began to find the witches. They had landed in all sorts of funny places. She helped three of them as they clambered out of bushes and trees. Two more climbed down from a haystack, and she brushed down their cloaks and pulled pieces of hay from their long black hair.

When she got to the market square she found one poor witch sitting in the water trough! She was wet through, of course, so Mildred kindly wrapped her own dry cloak around the shivering witch's shoulders.

Cold and very shaken after their nasty experience, they slowly made their way to Bubblepot's house. The Head Witch had landed safely and had already made a cauldron of hot brew. As the witches arrived they were given some brew and they clasped the steaming cups, grateful for some warmth. Mildred had some and felt pleased when Bubblepot thanked her for her help.

'It was good of you to turn out on such a night, Mildred,' she said. 'We shan't forget that you helped us.'

How lovely it was to be told she'd been useful! A warm glow spread around inside her, and Mildred knew it wasn't just the hot brew, but a nice feeling of belonging.

Soon the witches began to think of snug beds and a cosy cat to warm their feet. It had been quite a night and they all felt very tired.

They were just saying their 'Goodnight-and-thank-you's' to Bubblepot when a strange thing happened. A bright blue glow appeared in the sky. The witches stood still and watched it. The glow became a ball of light which came nearer and nearer.

They had never seen anything like it before and became rather excited. This was turning out to be a very unusual night! Bubblepot watched the blue light as it drew near. She thought she knew what it was, but said nothing until she was sure.

Then, just as the light seemed to fill the sky, a wonderful fairy-like figure appeared as if from nowhere. Straightaway Bubblepot said:

'I thought so . . . stand very still, all of you, and don't say a word. It's the Silver Witch, the Queen of the Night!'

The witches were terrified; the Silver Witch, the Queen of the Night! They'd heard of her, of course, but no one had seen her. Except Bubblepot, who had seen everything. The Silver Witch ruled over all the night lands. She knew every witch who'd ever ridden a broomstick. She also knew every witch who'd never ridden a broomstick, as we shall see! Only something very important could have brought her to such a small place as Thistleberry.

Without a sound the Silver Witch, the Queen of the Night, floated down and stood in front of them. Mildred had never seen anyone more beautiful.

She wore a silver dress that shimmered like moonbeams on a lake. Her great jewelled wings were folded beneath her cloak of silver silk and on her head was a crown of glittering diamonds. Her golden hair reached almost to the ground, and her eyes were like deep shining pools of morning dew. When Mildred looked at her eyes, she felt sure that the Queen of the Night knew everything there was to know in the whole world.

The witches were so amazed by the sight of her that they just stood and stared. Then Bubble-pot felt she ought to say something.

'Welcome, oh Queen!' she began. 'How kind of you to visit our poor village!'

The Queen of the Night said nothing. She was looking round at the group of witches, as if searching for someone.

Bubblepot had another try:

'Will you honour me by entering my humble abode?'

'Abode' sounded grander than 'home', and Bubblepot wanted everyone to see that she knew how you spoke to a queen.

'A glass of our best Thistleberry wine perhaps?' she asked.

The Head Witch was beginning to get a tiny bit cross at getting no answer, but of course she couldn't show it. Queens often took a long time about things, and you just had to put up with it.

At last the Queen of the Night turned to her and spoke in a clear silvery voice:

'Thank you, Head Witch,' she said with a shining smile, 'I have come on important business and I am sorry I cannot accept your invitation.'

Bubblepot gave a secret sigh of relief. Lovely as it would be to entertain the Queen of the Night, she'd had no time to tidy up and her house was in a bit of a pickle.

Once more the Queen of the Night looked round at the witches.

'I've come to see the small witch called Mildred,' she said. 'Is she here?'

Mildred couldn't believe her ears. Surely the Queen of the Night hadn't come all this way just to see her?

'Come along, Mildred!' said Bubblepot in a loud whisper. 'Don't keep the Queen waiting!'

Mildred walked forward, sure that she must be in a dream. She stood in front of the Queen.

'Ah, Mildred! Just the person I wanted!' said the Queen of the Night, looking her up and down. 'Yes, you're small enough. In fact, I think you'll do very nicely!'

Mildred had no idea what she'd do nicely for, but knew better than to ask.

'I need your help,' the Queen went on, 'I've got a bit of a problem and only a very small witch can sort it out for me.'

Mildred was too surprised for words. She could still hardly believe what was happening.

'I was out in my silver coach this evening,' explained the Queen. 'It was very windy, as you know . . .'

All the witches nodded at each other. Yes, they knew how windy it had been!

'. . . and I lost the biggest diamond in my crown. It must have been a bit loose,' said the Queen. 'And the wind blew it away. See! That's where it came from.'

The Queen of the Night pointed to the top of her crown, and, sure enough, there was a bit missing.

'I've found where it is,' said the Queen. 'It's fallen down a small hole in a cloud. I can see it gleaming but I can't reach it. That's why I need you, Mildred.'

'Need me?' Mildred's voice was small and scared. 'Need me for what? . . . Your Queen-ness,' she added politely.

Bubblepot gave a little 'tut-tut'. That was not at all what you called the Queen of the Night. Still, Mildred wasn't to know that.

The Queen seemed not to notice Mildred's mistake and said in a brisk voice:

'Why, to come up with me, squeeze down the hole in the cloud and rescue my diamond. Then you can fly back on your broomstick. Shouldn't be any problem for you, my dear!'

The Queen of the Night gave another of her

lovely smiles, until she saw Mildred's face, which had gone very white. Her knees knocked together and her lips trembled so that when the Queen asked:

'Whatever's the matter, Mildred?'

She could only stammer:

'I – I . . . c–c–can't! P–p–please, d–don't ask m–me! I c–c–can't!'

'Why ever not?' demanded the Queen of the Night.

Mildred was so upset at saying 'no' to the Queen, and so ashamed of her fear of flying, that she couldn't say anything. It was Bubblepot who explained all about Mildred's fears, her thin spindly broomstick, and everything. The Queen of the Night smiled kindly at Mildred.

'I do understand, my dear,' she said. 'In fact I've known for a long time that you are afraid to fly. But no one else is small enough to reach my diamond.' She paused thoughtfully. 'I'll tell you what. If you help me, I'll help you. That's fair, isn't it?'

'Yes, Your Nightiness,' whispered Mildred.

Bubblepot groaned very quietly. 'Nightiness' was even worse than 'Queen-ness'!

'Very well then,' said the Queen, trying to

hide a tiny smile. 'It's agreed. You know how you can help me. As to how I will help you; well, you'll have to wait and see!'

With that, she reached down, gathered Mildred and her broomstick in her arms, and held them firmly in the folds of her silver cloak. Before the witches had time to blink, they were gone, high up in the starry night!

Mildred closed her eyes and tried not to think of the ground, miles below her. She was safe in the Queen's cloak but even so it was a long way down!

Soon the wind stopped rushing past her face. They were slowing down, and Mildred opened her eyes. They landed on quite a big cloud which had a hole in its middle.

'There, Mildred!' said the Queen of the Night. 'Can you see my diamond gleaming?'

'Yes, Your Silverness,' replied Mildred, holding tightly to the Queen's hand. 'It's quite a long way inside, isn't it?'

'Yes, I know,' said the Queen. 'But I'm sure you can squeeze your way in. Come on Mildred, be brave! I'll hold your broomstick.'

'I will be brave!' Mildred told herself, 'I really will!'

And she let go of the Queen's hand and pushed herself head first into the hole. It got dark very quickly but Mildred could see the diamond shining in front of her. She kept pushing herself forward. Oh it was so stuffy, and nasty cobwebs caught on her face!

'Have you got it yet?' called the Queen of the Night. Her voice sounded a long way off.

'Not yet!' Mildred shouted back. She pushed and pushed until at last the diamond was almost within her grasp. She touched it! She nearly grabbed it! Then it slipped.

'Oh no!' she gasped. 'No, it can't!'

The diamond stopped sliding and Mildred wormed her way forward once more. Almost . . . a bit further . . . she touched it . . . she held it!

'I've got it! I've got it!' she called.

'Oh well done, Mildred!' The Queen sounded overjoyed. 'Now push backwards until I can get hold of your feet and pull you out. And please don't drop the diamond!'

Mildred wriggled and squirmed back the way she had come. Then she felt the Queen's hands on her feet. Gently the Queen pulled, and soon Mildred was out in the fresh air once more. She gave the diamond to the Queen of the Night.

'Thank you, Mildred. I am very proud of you!' said the Queen. 'Now, your Head Witch will be wondering where you are. It's time you flew home on your broomstick.'

Mildred's knees began to wobble again. She had felt so important and pleased at helping the Queen of the Night. Now the thought of flying on her thin spindly broomstick spoiled every-thing.

'I'm sorry, Your Wonderfulness,' she whis-pered. 'But I can't fly home. I'm frightened.'

'I promised I would help you, Mildred,' said the Queen of the Night, 'I think this will make flying a bit easier.'

As she spoke she handed Mildred her broomstick. The little witch looked at it; she looked at it again. Her eyes nearly popped out of her head! Gone was the thin spindly broomstick and, in its place, she held the biggest strongest one she had ever seen!

'Oh! Oh my stars!' she gasped. 'Is it really for me? Is it?'

'Of course it is!' said the Queen of the Night with a smile. 'It's my way of saying "thank you" for helping me.'

Mildred gazed and gazed at the beautiful broomstick. It was what she wanted more than anything else.

'But I've still got to fly on it, haven't I?' she said to the Queen. 'And I'm still afraid of flying!'

'I'm sure you are,' answered the Queen, 'but remember that your magic will be much stronger now that you have your new broomstick. With that, and my help, I don't think you'll be afraid for long!'

'Oh, I do hope not!' she said, still worried.

'Come on, Mildred!' the Queen's voice was

firm. 'You'll never know if you don't try, will you?'

'No, I suppose I won't,' agreed the little witch.

She went to the edge of the cloud and sat on the new broomstick. It certainly felt a lot safer.

'Off you go, Mildred!' called the Queen of the Night. 'Be brave and fly quickly home!'

'Goodbye!' Mildred called back, 'and thank you for my broomstick!'

Then she had a sudden thought.

'Will I ever see you again, Your Silverness?' she asked.

The Queen of the Night smiled.

'Perhaps you will, one day,' she said. 'Now fly, Mildred, fly!'

And the little witch gripped the wonderful broomstick, closed her eyes, and sprang off the edge of the cloud into the night sky.

For a moment she was afraid. Then she opened her eyes and saw the friendly stars winking at her as she raced by.

'I'm flying! I'm really flying!' she called to them, 'I'm not afraid any more!'

She turned to look back at the cloud. She could just see the Queen of the Night, her shining hair and her silken cloak blowing round her in the gentle breeze.

Mildred waved to her. The Queen waved back and whispered across the open sky:

'Good luck, you brave little witch!'

Soon Mildred was flying over Thistleberry.

'Home!' she thought, 'I'm home at last!'

Far below, she saw Bubblepot and the other witches gazing up to look for her. When they caught sight of her on her amazing new broomstick, they all began to wave excitedly.

'How kind of them all to wait for me!' she said to herself. 'And I can't wait, I simply can't wait to tell them that flying is the most wonderful thing in the world!'

# The Giant's Handkerchief

It was a bright, beautiful morning. Amelia made her bed and washed up her breakfast dishes in the pool of rainwater by the back door. She dried them on a clean cobweb and prepared her basket of cakes for the dragon, then set off through the village towards the hill where he lived.

Soon she had left the houses behind and began to climb the steep path which led up the hill to the dragon's cave. She stopped once or twice to pick wild flowers and to give her legs a rest. You could have run up that hill without even getting puffed, but Amelia was very small so it wasn't quite so easy for her.

When she stopped the second time, she sat down on the grass to admire the view. On such a clear day you could see right over Thistleberry, far away to the hills.

Then she heard an odd noise for such a lovely day. Someone was crying, and whoever it was seemed quite near as the sound was very loud. She heard some sniffing and a 'drip-tap, drip-tap' noise, like rain falling into a puddle.

'Oh dear,' thought Amelia. 'This won't do. I'd better see if I can help.'

The sound came from behind an enormous tree near the path. She crept over and peeped round its trunk. She was amazed! There, in the middle of a huge pool of water, was the biggest foot she had ever seen, in a brown boot the size of her house! Amelia peeped round a bit more, and there was another brown boot, exactly like the first.

The crying noise was coming from high over her head and she was just about to look up when 'Splat!' Something hit her on the head with a bang which knocked her right over. She picked herself up and found that her hair was soaking wet.

'Bother!' she said crossly. 'I've already washed my hair this morning, and it had dried quite nicely in the sunshine. Now it's all wet again!'

'I'm sorry!' said a deep rumbling voice, way up high. 'I'm so unhappy I just can't stop crying.'

54

Amelia looked up. She saw a pair of green trousers. She looked up further and saw a green jacket. Then she put her head back as far as she could. Right up on top of the jacket was a red, crying face. Some more tear drops fell and Amelia jumped out of the way before she got wet again.

'Hallo!' she called up, 'I'm Amelia. Who are you, and why are you crying such a lot?'

'I'm Jack Greenjacket,' sniffed the red, crying face. 'I'm a giant . . . sniff, sniff . . . and I'm crying . . . sniff, sniff . . . because I've lost my best red spotted hanky.'

'Oh dear!' said Amelia as she jumped round to find a dry bit of ground. 'I am sorry to hear that. Haven't you got another hanky?'

Jack Greenjacket put his hand in his pocket and pulled out a crumpled green cloth with white spots.

'Yes, I have got another one,' he sniffed. 'But it's far too wet to use. And I don't like the colour.'

He started to squeeze the green handkerchief and so much water came down that Amelia wished she had brought her umbrella. She suggested they dry the handkerchief in the sunshine,

which made Jack stop crying for a while. Having someone to talk to had brightened him up a bit.

He told Amelia that he was on his way to visit his uncle. Last night he had settled down to sleep under the big tree, and when he woke that morning, the red spotted handkerchief had gone. It was his favourite thing in the whole world.

'You see,' he explained to Amelia, 'I get fed up with having everything green. I've got a green jacket, green trousers and green socks.'

'But how smart!' said Amelia, 'I mean, to have everything matching.'

'Huh!' said Jack crossly. 'It may be smart to you, but a giant can get fed up with it, you know. Green! Green! Green! I hate green! That's why I loved my red spotted hanky so much!'

'Yes, I do see what you mean,' said Amelia, who loved to wear lots of different colours. 'It must be very upsetting for you.'

The giant began to cry again, and Amelia wished she had learned to swim. She had to do something to help him.

'I'll tell you what, Jack,' she said, adding politely, 'May I call you Jack?'

He nodded through his tears.

'I'll tell you what; when I've taken my cakes to the dragon, we'll both go back to Thistleberry and we'll ask everyone to help look for your red spotted hanky.'

So Amelia hurried off. The dragon was not very pleased at such a rushed visit as he enjoyed a good chat in the mornings. Amelia explained about Jack Greenjacket and promised to stay longer the next day. Soon she was back at the tree.

Jack looked quite a lot brighter, and together they went back to Thistleberry. Amelia had a job keeping up with Jack's long strides and was really tired by the time they reached the village.

In Thistleberry the news about Jack Green-jacket soon spread and everyone gathered in the market place to meet him. They felt sorry for him and promised to help. Someone asked him exactly what his handkerchief looked like, so they would know what they were searching for. Jack told them it was big and bright red, with lovely white spots all over it. The thought of it made him sad and he started to cry again.

His teardrops fell in a heavy downpour and everyone ran for cover. As he cried, the pool of water at his feet got bigger and bigger. Soon the market place was flooded and the nearby streets started to fill up. The village pond disappeared in the rush of water and everyone got very worried. If the red spotted handkerchief wasn't found quickly, they might all drown.

So anyone who had a boat set off to look for the handkerchief. The others stayed indoors and kept an eye on the rising flood. As he didn't know his way round Thistleberry, it was agreed that Jack should stay in the market place while the search went on. All the time, he kept crying and crying.

Amelia was the first to hurry away. She hadn't got a boat, and she knew she must search the dry places before the water spread. She had a feeling that the red spotted handkerchief wasn't in the village, or it would have been found by now. She decided to look in the farmer's fields.

She came to the barn where the cows slept and went inside. She was rather afraid of cows and kept looking over her shoulder in case one should come in. She peered under the water trough. She burrowed under the bales of hay, which was a very scratchy place to look. But there was no sign of the handkerchief.

When she came out of the barn, the sky had gone very dark. As if things weren't wet enough, it was going to rain! The first raindrops began to fall, slowly at first, then faster and faster. Soon Amelia's hair was soaked, for the third time that day, and her clothes were wet through. Her little feet squelched through the muddy field. That red spotted handkerchief had got to be found, and very soon!

She ran through the fields as fast as she could, her wet dress clinging to her legs. It felt horrible!

Then Amelia heard someone calling her name. She stopped. The voice was coming from up in the air.

'Amelia! Amelia!'

She looked up and saw Kerry the Kingfisher. He flew down and landed on the squashy ground. His coloured feathers looked dark and bedraggled from the heavy rain.

'Thank goodness I've found you!' he said. 'The village people sent me to warn you that the floods are coming this way. You must get back or you'll be cut off from Thistleberry!'

'I'll come back very soon, Kerry,' said Amelia, 'I must just check the field across the river. It's the only place I haven't looked for the hanky.'

'All right, if you think there's time,' said Kerry, 'but don't be long. I'd stay and help you but I've got to make sure there's no one else in danger.'

'Thank you for coming to find me,' said Amelia, 'I won't be long. Tell me,' she added, 'is Jack Greenjacket still crying?'

'I'm afraid so,' replied Kerry. 'If he doesn't stop soon, I don't know what will happen. Well, goodbye, Amelia, and be careful!'

He flew away and Amelia hurried towards the river. All she had to do was look over to the field on the other side where the wood fairies lived. If there was no sign of the handkerchief, she would go straight back to Thistleberry.

When she reached the river, what a sight met her eyes! It had burst its banks on the side she was on, and a flood of water raced towards her. Amelia was scared.

'There's no time to check the field on the other side,' she thought, 'I must go back to the village now!'

But she'd left it too late. There was a rushing sound behind her and, when she looked, a wave of flood water was getting nearer and nearer. She was surrounded by water, and there was no escape!

'Oh, I wish I'd gone back when Kerry told me to!' she thought. 'Now what am I to do?'

Just by the river bank, or where it would be if it weren't under water, there was a tree.

'It's my only hope!' she muttered desperately, 'I must climb it before I'm swallowed up in the floods!'

She sploshed over the wet ground and managed to scramble up to the first branch. It was very difficult as the tree was slippery with rain. Amelia sat on the branch and looked down. By now the water was swishing around the bottom of the tree. It kept on rising. She must get up higher.

Very carefully, putting her tiny hands and feet into small dents in the bark, she inched her way up. Once she nearly slipped off, and her heart banged in fear. Using all her strength, which

wasn't much, she clambered on to the branch
above and sat astride it. She was safe, at least for
the moment.

'Now I'll just have to wait for the water to go
down!' she thought, trying to keep cheerful.

But it kept on raining, and Amelia got very
cold in her thin wet dress. How she longed to be
home in her little warm house.

She had almost forgotten the red spotted
handkerchief. When she did think of it, she
looked across the river but it was too misty to see
the field.

Poor Amelia! She was wet, cold and stuck up a

tree. And she hadn't found the handkerchief. What an awful day!

At last the rain stopped, but the flood water would take a long time to go down, especially if Jack Greenjacket was still crying! Amelia realised she could be in the tree all night. She was very miserable and felt like crying.

'But that will just make more water!' she murmured, and held back her tears.

At last, just when she had given up hope of ever being on the ground again, she heard loud sploshy footsteps approaching. It was Jack Greenjacket! He'd come to look for her!

'Jack! Jack!' she called, 'I'm up here!'

Jack saw her, waved and came over to the tree. He was so tall that the flood water hardly reached his knees!

'Oh, I'm so pleased to see you, Jack!' cried Amelia, 'And . . . you've stopped crying!'

'Well, I was so worried about you,' said Jack, 'it made me forget about my hanky. After all, you've been a good friend, and a friend is much more important than a hanky! The kingfisher said you must be near the river, so I came to find you.'

As he spoke, he lifted Amelia out of the tree.

Of course, being so big, he didn't even have to stretch up! She sat on his shoulder and looked around. The mist had cleared and she had a wonderful view. She happened to look across the river to the field beyond. Something unusual caught her eye.

'Whatever's that?' she said. 'It looks like a huge tablecloth!'

Jack looked to where she was pointing. In the field the wood fairies had come out, and they were spreading an enormous red spotted cloth on the grass.

'That's not a tablecloth!' exclaimed Jack. 'That's my hanky! Oh Amelia, we've found it!'

He carried her across the river as easily as if it were a puddle. The wood fairies had begun to dance on the handkerchief, jumping from one white spot to another. They stopped in terror when they saw Jack coming. Their faces went very red.

'We didn't mean any harm, Sir!' they cried. 'We only borrowed your handkerchief while you were asleep. You see, it's so good for dancing on!'

Jack was so pleased the handkerchief was found that he wasn't really cross at all.

Together they all, folded up the red spotted handkerchief and Jack put it in his pocket. He looked at the wood fairies' sad faces. They were quite right: the spots on the bright cloth had made perfect patterns for marking their dancing positions. He put his hand in his other pocket.

'I'll tell you what,' he said, 'I don't need two hankies. Why don't you have my green one? You can dance on it just as well and it will match the grass!'

'Oh! Yes please!' shouted the fairies. They were thrilled.

They spread the green spotted handkerchief out on the field. In no time they were dancing again, with their band blowing a lively tune. Amelia and Jack watched them as they jumped in and out of the white spots.

Amelia was still cold and rather hungry, so it wasn't long before she asked Jack to take her back to the village. They said goodbye to the wood fairies, who thanked Jack once more, and promised they would never take anyone's handkerchief again, or even borrow it, without asking.

Soon Jack was carrying Amelia back to Thistleberry. The evening sun smiled down on them and the flood water was quickly going down.

'It really was kind of you, Jack,' said Amelia, 'I mean, to give the wood fairies your green hanky.'

'Well, why not?' said Jack happily, 'After all, my day turned out very well in the end. I found my red spotted hanky and, something even better, I found a very good friend!'

Amelia said nothing, but she smiled all the way home.

# Musty and the Big Blue Toad

You'd hardly believe it to look at her now, but
Bubblepot the Head Witch was once a beautiful,
slender young thing. This was a very long time
ago, of course, when her grandmother was Head
Witch. Granny was very keen that Bubblepot
should become successful and important.

'And there's one thing you do need, my dear,'
she would croak. 'You must have a cat. You
really must have a cat.'

She said this so often that the words seemed to
sing in Bubblepot's head.

'Must-have-a-cat. Must-have-a-cat.'

So when she got her cat and was wondering
what to call it, Granny's words kept coming
back to her.

'Must-have-a-cat. Must-have-a-cat.'

So she joined all the words together to make

the name 'Mustapha Cat', or 'Musty' for short.

Musty wasn't all that fond of his name. It sounded rather dull and cobwebby, but once you've got a name, there's nothing you can do about it. Like it or not, you're stuck with it.

As we know, Bubblepot did indeed become successful and important. When she was made Head Witch, she didn't have many hard spells to make because she could always ask the other witches to do them for her. So she became just a little bit lazy and just a little bit fat, though of course no one dared say so.

And Musty became rather fat and lazy too. There was no need to go hunting for bats and snails for his mistress's spells, so he spent most of his time dozing in the armchair by the fire. It was so lovely to sleep a bit, wake up to stretch your claws, have a little something to drink and go back to sleep again.

One day Bubblepot was sitting in front of her mirror. She was feeling bored. She looked at her hooked nose. She looked at her pointed chin. And she looked at her long black hair. She didn't like what she saw.

'I'm looking very ordinary and unexciting,' she thought. 'What I need is a change, something

to perk me up a bit. For a Head Witch, I'm very uninteresting. What do you think, Musty?'

But Musty was fast asleep in the armchair.

Then Bubblepot had a brilliant idea. She fetched her latest copy of 'News and Brews', the witches' magazine full of up-to-date handy hints. She rustled through the pages.

'It's in here somewhere,' she said. 'I'm sure I read it only last week . . . Ah ha! Here we are! Musty! Musty! Come and listen to this!'

Musty yawned, stretched and wandered slowly over to his mistress.

'Did you want me?' he said, still half asleep.

'Yes! Yes!' cried Bubblepot excitedly. 'There's a spell in "News and Brews" to turn one's hair a beautiful blue. I'm going to try it!'

'Oh no!' thought Musty. 'Not blue hair! She'll look dreadful!'

'Now I need your help,' Bubblepot went on. 'I've got almost everything I need to make the spell, but I must have another Big Blue Toad.'

Musty's eyes were beginning to close but the Head Witch was too excited to notice.

'Luckily I caught one hopping round the garden a couple of days ago,' she went on. 'The silly thing must have got lost. They don't usually come this far from the river. It's safely in my toad box in the spell cupboard, so you only need to find one. Are you listening, Musty?'

Musty was fast asleep on the carpet.

'Wake up, you lazy thing!' shouted Bubblepot. 'Make yourself useful for once. Go and find me a Big Blue Toad!'

Musty opened one eye.

'But I loathe toads!' he moaned. 'Especially Big Blue ones. They're so slippery and difficult to catch!'

'Bosh!' cried his mistress. 'You could catch one easily enough if you weren't so fat and lazy!'

'Look who's talking!' muttered Musty. It was a good thing Bubblepot didn't hear what he said.

'Now you'll have to be quick,' she told him. 'The Big Blue Toad in my spell box is starting to lose its colour so we haven't much time.'

She picked up the cat and pushed him out of the door.

'Off you go!' she said, 'While I prepare the other things I need. I'll have the first Big Blue Toad all ready for the boiling pot by the time you get back!'

Musty wandered off through Thistleberry, wishing he were back in the armchair. He saw a mouse which scuttled out of his way, and a large brown snail who quickly popped into its shell. But Musty couldn't be bothered with either of them. Then he met his friend Lancelot who was cleaning his whiskers by the side of the road.

'Well, bless my paws, it's Musty!' called Lancelot. 'Don't tell me old Bubblepot has actually sent you out to work! What are you hunting for?'

'A Big Blue Toad, if you must know,' answered Musty.

'Now, I may be able to help you with that,' said Lancelot. 'I saw one jumping around by the river only this morning. What do you want it for?'

Musty went up close and whispered something in his friend's ear.

'You can't be serious!' said Lancelot in amazement. 'But that's terrible! What will she look like?'

'Doesn't bear thinking about,' said Musty, and wandered off towards the river.

He stopped several times for a cat-nap, and then realised it was getting late. He found a good hiding place with a clear view of the river bank. He tucked his hind legs under him in a ready-to-pounce sort of way, and waited. He seemed to wait a long time. His legs were getting stiff and his eyelids began to droop.

Then there was a splashing at the water's edge. He heard some gulping and croaking and then, out from the shallows, came the biggest Big Blue Toad he had ever seen.

Musty was now wide awake, his eyes narrow as slits and his claws at the ready. His tail flicked from side to side as he watched. He had to choose just the right moment to pounce.

The Big Blue Toad was looking around and croaking loudly, as if calling to someone. For a second his back was turned. Musty sprang at him. The Big Blue Toad saw him just in time and

leapt back into the water. He sat on the leaves of a
huge water lily and called out:

'You'll have to be quicker than that, you fat
black cat!'

Musty had pounced so quickly he almost
toppled into the river.

'Now that's not fair!' he called. 'You know I
can't get you while you're in the water. You're
cheating!'

'No I'm not!' replied the Big Blue Toad. 'I just
don't want to be caught!'

'But I need you,' said Musty. 'At least, my
mistress does. She's got one Big Blue Toad but
she wants another for her boiling pot.'

'What!' cried the Big Blue Toad. 'Did you say

she already got one like me? Oh no! It must be Gertrude!'

'Who on earth is Gertrude?' asked Musty. Time was slipping by and Bubblepot would be getting impatient.

'Gertrude's my wife, and I'm George,' replied the Big Blue Toad. 'She's been missing for days and I've called and called her. And you say your mistress is going to boil her? Oh, this is awful!'

'Yes, isn't it?' said Musty, not in the least bit bothered. 'And she's going to boil you as well!'

George was silent for a moment. Things were looking rather tricky and he needed to think carefully. After a while he asked why Bubblepot needed to boil two Big Blue Toads. Musty explained about the blue hair, and George began to jump up and down on the water lily.

'But she doesn't need to boil us!' he cried excitedly. 'Believe me, all she has to do is put us in warm water. Then, if she says the spell and puts her head in the water with us, it will work perfectly!'

'It's a trick!' said Musty. 'You just don't want to be boiled!'

'Of course I don't!' said George. 'But it isn't that, I promise you. My plan really will work!'

Musty wasn't at all sure.

'Oh please trust me!' pleaded George. 'And we must hurry, or it will be too late for dear Gertrude!'

Musty wasn't really bothered about dear Gertrude. He just sat on the river bank, thinking things over.

Then he made up his mind.

'All right!' he said. 'We'll go back and tell Bubblepot she needn't boil you. But I warn you . . .' and he waved his paw at George, 'if this is a trick, I'll get her to boil you twice!'

So they hurried back to the Head Witch's house. George kept to the river, leaping from one water lily to the next, just in case the cat should pounce on him after all. Musty ran along the river bank, keeping a close watch on the Big Blue Toad. Every few hops George would call out:

'Hurry! Hurry! Oh Gertrude! I only hope we're in time!'

At last they reached the house and found Bubblepot standing over an enormous boiling pot. She was stirring it with a long wooden spoon. With her other hand she lowered a trembling Big Blue Toad towards the hot bubbles.

George shouted in horror:

'Oh no! Please stop! You mustn't boil Gertrude!'

Bubblepot turned to him.

'Ah ha,' she cried. 'The other one! You're just in time!'

'Stop, mistress! Stop!' gasped Musty, quite out of breath after such a run.

'Dear me, Musty!' said Bubblepot. 'It's a disgrace to be so unfit! Now what's all this about Gertrude, and why mustn't I boil her?'

Still puffing and panting, Musty explained about George, Gertrude and George's plan.

'Oh I don't think that would work at all!' she said when Musty had finished. 'No, I'm sorry but I really must boil both of them.'

She put Gertrude so close to the steaming water that her little blue feet almost touched it.

'Goodbye, dear George!' she called, lifting a webbed foot to wipe away her tears.

George was desperate.

'Please!' he shouted to Bubblepot. 'Please, just give my plan a try! It can't do any harm. If it doesn't work, then you can boil us!'

The Head Witch thought about this for quite a long time. Gertrude could hardly be seen through all the steam, and George was afraid in case she couldn't breathe. At last Bubblepot spoke:

'Very well then!' she agreed grumpily. 'I suppose we could give it a go.'

She put Gertrude down on the floor.

'Oh thank you!' cried both Big Blue Toads. What a relief it was to know they would not be boiled, at least not yet!

Bubblepot moved the boiling pot away from the fire and waited for it to cool down a bit. She added the other secret bits and pieces to the water and then tested it with her finger.

'All right,' she said, 'It's ready.'

George and Gertrude hopped on to the edge of the pot. They balanced there for a moment, counted down from ten, and plunged in.

'Oh!' squeaked Gertrude. 'It's lovely! Just like a warm bath!'

George gave a show of his best frog stroke, swimming so fast that he was just a blue streak whizzing round the pot.

'Come along, come along! That's enough of that!' called Bubblepot. 'You're not here to play, you know!'

The Big Blue Toads kept still while Bubblepot

closed her eyes and spoke the words of the spell:

*Oggle, Boggle, Stir and Stew,*
*Make my hair turn bright bright blue!'*

'Now put your head in the water,' said George.

Bubblepot knelt down and bent over the pot.

'Now don't jump on my head, you two!' she said to the Big Blue Toads. 'I simply couldn't bear it.'

She held her nose and put her head right into the water with George and Gertrude.

Musty didn't know whether he wanted the spell to work or not. He didn't want his mistress to have blue hair, and yet he didn't want the toads to be boiled.

For a moment nothing happened and it seemed as if George's plan wouldn't work. Then the water began to gurgle and froth. Large blue bubbles blobbed up round Bubblepot's head. She held her breath for as long as she could, then came up gasping and spluttering.

'Has it worked? Tell me if it's worked!'

Musty looked at her hair. It was still as black as before.

'Er . . . well . . . not quite, mistress,' he said, already feeling sorry for George and Gertrude.

'What!' screamed Bubblepot. 'It's either worked or it hasn't, you stupid cat!'

Not caring about her wet hair dripping on the floor, she rushed over to the mirror. When she saw her black hair she was furious.

'I'll boil you! I'll boil you!' she shouted, and grabbed George and Gertrude. The poor Big Blue Toads were terrified. It was to be Toad Hot Pot after all. Musty felt very sad. He had grown quite fond of them and it seemed such a pity. Just as Bubblepot was about to throw them back in the water and reheat the pot, Musty caught sight of her hair. It had begun to change colour!

'Wait, mistress!' he called, 'I think the spell's working!'

The Head Witch dropped the poor toads on the floor and ran back to the mirror. Sure enough, her hair was turning blue. As she watched, it got brighter and brighter until it was just like a summer sky. And just as Musty had feared, it looked dreadful.

'Oh, that's perfect!' said Bubblepot, 'I look absolutely beautiful!'

'That's what you think!' muttered Musty under his breath.

George and Gertrude hopped over to get a good look.

'Don't you think it's splendid?' Bubblepot asked them.

George didn't know what to say, but Gertrude was very tactful.

'I'm simply lost for words!' she said. Bubble-pot was delighted.

'Well, thank you both,' she said. 'You were quite right after all, and you've saved me a lot of boiling bother!'

'Only too glad to help out,' said George. 'Do call on us again if you need us. Now we must be on our way.'

They all said goodbye and the Big Blue Toads hopped back to their home by the river.

Musty settled himself in the armchair and closed his eyes. He'd had a very busy day and was quite worn out. Bubblepot pranced round the room in excitement and then went back to admire herself in the mirror.

'There's no doubt about it,' she said. 'It really suits me. I think I might try all sorts of different colours in turn. What do you think, Musty? How about a wonderful pink?'

'Oh no!' thought Musty, 'Not pink! I couldn't stand it!'

And he pretended to be fast asleep.

# Bubblepot's Birthday

Bubblepot was the Head Witch in Thistleberry. She was very jolly, with a voice which gurgled like a bubbling cauldron. She was a kind witch, but could be very strict if anyone did anything wrong. She made all the rules about spells, and that meant she was very important.

As you know, bad witches were not allowed in the village, so whenever a witch came to Thistleberry she had to go and see Bubblepot. The new witch would take her two books of spells. One was for good spells and the other for bad spells.

Bubblepot would look through the good spells to make sure they really were all right. Then the new witch was allowed to take her good spell book and live in the village. After she'd gone, Bubblepot would take the book of bad spells and hide it away in a secret place which no one else knew about.

This plan worked very well and the people of Thistleberry knew that they need never be afraid of the witches, who had no power to make nasty things happen because they didn't know where their bad spell books were.

One day, however, a really bad witch came to the village and things started to go wrong.

Her name was Slimyweed. It was a good name for her because she was a slippery sort of person, thin and greenish like the seaweed you find on wet rocks.

When she was much younger, her mother, who was an even nastier witch than Slimyweed, had given her a magic cloak. When she put it on she became invisible, so she had great fun putting all sorts of horrible spells on people, without anyone seeing her.

Slimyweed had heard that Thistleberry was a happy village and that no bad witches were allowed to live there. She hated happy places; they weren't any fun. So she came to Thistleberry with one thing in mind, and that was to make trouble.

She knocked on Bubblepot's front door just

after lunch. The Head Witch was having a sleep after her meal and was awakened by the noise. She hurried to put on her purple dress with the silver moons and opened the door.

'Good afternoon,' she said, looking closely at Slimyweed, because she'd never seen her before.

'How do you do?' replied Slimyweed in a slithery sort of voice, 'I've just come to Thistleberry and I've brought you my spell books.'

'I see,' said Bubblepot in a business-like sort of way. 'Well, do come in and sit down and I'll have a look at them.'

She didn't much like the look of Slimyweed, but if her bad spell book was taken away, she couldn't do any harm. Bubblepot lifted her big black cat out of the armchair and Slimyweed sat down. She took the two spell books from her bag, taking care to leave her magic cloak tucked out of sight at the bottom.

Bubblepot looked quickly through the good spell book. There was nothing much to worry about in there, as all the spells appeared quite harmless.

'That seems to be in order,' she said, handing the book back to Slimyweed. 'Now let me see the bad spells.'

She was very shocked at what she found. There really were some very unpleasant tricks in that book, and the sooner it was safely out of the way, the better for everyone.

'Yes, well, we won't be needing those, will we?' she said in an un-bothered way so that Slimyweed wouldn't know how bothered she really was.

'I'll look after this book in a safe place. Off you go then. Oh yes, and I hope you'll enjoy living here.' She thought she'd better say that, just to be polite.

Slimyweed stood up and put the good spell book in her bag. She smiled a nasty smile and said:

'Oh I'm sure I'll have a very good time in Thistleberry!'

Of course Bubblepot didn't know what she meant by that. If she had known, she would have been very worried.

As soon as she had walked down the front path and was hidden by the hedge, Slimyweed quickly put on her magic cloak. She just wasn't there! Well, she was, but no one could see her!

She ran round the house to Bubblepot's back door and crept in. She was just in time to see the

Head Witch pick up the book of bad spells. She had a good look round the room and out of the windows to make sure no one was watching her. Slimyweed was standing right next to her, but she didn't know that!

Bubblepot went over to her huge stone fireplace. She bent down, put her fingers in the small gaps around one of the big stones, and pulled. It wasn't easy because her fingers were rather fat to squeeze into the space, and the stone was heavy. After a lot of puffing and panting, she lifted the stone away. There was a big hole underneath, and it was full of bad spell books!

Slimyweed watched carefully as Bubblepot put her book in with the rest and heaved the stone back into place. The fireplace looked just as before and you would never have guessed what lay underneath.

Slimyweed tip-toed away through the back door and didn't take off her magic cloak until she was safely back in her own house. Then, there she was again! She thought of the fun she was going to have, and gave a horrid, cackling laugh.

Bubblepot soon forgot about Slimyweed and what an unpleasant witch she seemed. The bad spell book was out of reach, and anyway, she had more exciting things to think about. It was soon to be her birthday, and being a very important Head Witch didn't stop you looking forward very much to birthdays.

There would be a big party and she would invite all the witches she knew. Best of all would be the special birthday stew, full of her favourite food, like pink bats and snail juice. It would all be boiled up in an enormous cauldron in the garden. It was going to be so lovely, she really couldn't think about anything else.

Slimyweed could only think about one thing as well, but it wasn't birthdays. Day by day she kept a watch on the Head Witch's house, and wore her magic cloak so as not to be seen. She soon found that Bubblepot went out shopping every morning at twenty-past ten. Doing things at special times is very important to a witch. They learn this when they are young and never forget it.

One morning when she had seen Bubblepot leave the house with her shopping bag, Slimyweed went quietly up the path. There was one front window which didn't shut properly, and she was able to pull it open. She climbed up on to the ledge and squeezed through.

At that moment a young goblin walked by. He couldn't see Slimyweed, of course, but he did see the window opening, as if by itself. He ran off in a fright because he knew whose house it was. Windows don't open on their own unless by magic, and goblins are afraid of witch's magic.

Had the goblin not run off so quickly, he

might have caught a glimpse of Slimyweed because, a moment later, her magic cloak caught on the window latch and slipped from her shoulders. For a second she could be seen! She put the cloak back on straightaway and disappeared once more.

She went over to the fireplace and grasped the big stone in her bony fingers. Although she was thin, she was very strong, and soon lifted the stone away. She picked up the bad spell book on top of the pile and checked inside to make sure it was hers. It was. As fast as she could she put the stone back in its place and climbed out through the same window, her bad spell book hidden under the cloak.

By the time Bubblepot came home, her shopping bag full of good things for her party, Slimyweed was already back in her own house.

The bad witch sat up all night, searching her book of bad spells for the one she wanted. There were hundreds to look through, but at last she found the right one.

She went down to her kitchen and stood in the middle of the magic circle she always had ready on the floor. Holding the bad spell book in her skinny fingers, she sang in a horrid voice:

*'When you try to boil your pot,*
*All your spells will be forgot!'*

Of course it should have been 'forgotten', but that didn't rhyme with 'pot' and Slimyweed knew you had to follow the book exactly if the spell was to work.

Making spells is rather tiring work, and Slimyweed went back to bed for a good sleep. She laughed to herself, knowing she had already spoiled Bubblepot's party before it had even happened!

The day of her birthday came at last. Bubblepot was up early to open her cards and presents. Every witch had sent something, as it was very rude not to, and it might mean they wouldn't be invited to her party next year.

There were bat-wing cards, wands of every colour, black magic chocolates and even some oil for her broomstick.

'How thoughtful of them all!' Bubblepot said to herself as the presents piled up.

Soon all the witches arrived for the party. They wore their best gowns, but of course they said that Bubblepot looked the most beautiful. They had to say that partly because it was her birthday, and also because it was not wise to risk upsetting her.

They did a bit of dancing and flew around on their broomsticks before tea. Then the moment came for Bubblepot to light the fire under the huge cauldron. They were all looking forward to that lovely birthday stew.

Bubblepot stood by the huge pile of sticks and opened her mouth to say the spell which would set them alight. Everyone waited. They waited and waited, but she didn't say a word.

'What's the matter?' asked someone.

'It's awful!' said Bubblepot, 'I can't light the fire! I've forgotten the spell!'

She had another go, but again the spell wouldn't come. Some of the other witches tried, but it was no good. What on earth could they do? No fire meant no stew, and that would ruin the party.

They were so busy trying to think of another way to light the fire that no one heard the slow, careful footsteps creeping up close to the cauldron. They certainly couldn't see anything, because it was Slimyweed in her magic cloak. She'd had an invitation like everyone else, and had been there all the time, but of course no one had noticed her.

Now Slimyweed wanted to get near to see what Bubblepot would do. Her horrid plan was working perfectly!

Then one of the witches had a brilliant idea. It was so clever that Bubblepot was rather cross she hadn't thought of it herself. If someone would fetch that fairy called Amelia, she could ask the dragon to come and light the fire with one of his big puffs!

Of course they'd have to invite Amelia and the dragon to stay for the birthday stew, and it was really a party for witches only. However, they all thought that it wouldn't matter, just this once.

So a witch rushed off on her broomstick. She flew much faster than Bubblepot usually allowed but, after all, it was an emergency. Amelia agreed to ask the dragon for his help and the witch gave her a lift up to his cave.

Amelia held on tight and closed her eyes. She'd never flown on a broomstick before and it didn't feel very safe. Soon they arrived at the dragon's cave and Amelia hopped thankfully off the broomstick and went inside.

The dragon was none too pleased at being disturbed, but the promise of birthday stew sent him hurrying down to Bubblepot's garden.

Amelia and the witch flew back together, in time to see everyone clearing a space for the dragon to get near the cauldron.

He took a deep breath, and blew. It worked beautifully! The fire from his breath caught the smaller sticks and soon flames were burning merrily. It wasn't long before the birthday stew began to boil.

And where was Slimyweed? Well, she started to creep away from the cauldron just before the dragon began to puff out fire. She had only run a few steps when a large spark leapt out from the burning sticks and landed on her magic cloak. In a moment it was in flames!

As you can imagine, Slimyweed threw off the cloak very quickly before it became a pile of ashes. She didn't want to burn, but now of course everyone could see her! And in her hand was the bad spell book which she hadn't dared to leave behind. Bubblepot shouted at her. The witches had never heard her sound so angry.

'You! Slimyweed!' she called. 'Come here at once!'

Slimyweed obeyed. Bubblepot saw the bad spell book and guessed at once what had happened.

'I never did like the look of you!' she cried, 'and your wicked plan nearly spoiled my birthday!'

Her voice sounded like thunder, and every witch trembled in fright.

'Your bad spell made me forget my good fire-lighting one. Now you will put things to rights!'

Even Slimyweed, bad as she was, shook with fright at such fury.

'A spell now, if you please!' ordered Bubblepot. 'A spell to bring back my memory!'

The bad witch had to think for a moment, because she hadn't got her good spell book with her. Then she spoke these words:

'*Shake the mind and poke the ember,*
*Once again you will remember!*'

Everyone held their breath. Would the good spell work? Then, as easily as if she'd known it all the time, Bubblepot said:

'*Boki, Doki, twist and turn,*
*Flames to sticks and fire burn!*'

Of course the fire was already alight, thanks to the dragon, but at Bubblepot's words, new flames leapt up round the cauldron, bigger and brighter than before. The stew was very nearly ready, but before they all sat down, the Head Witch had one more thing to do.

'Slimyweed!' she said, 'Your magic cloak has gone, and you are to give me your book of bad spells!'

Slimyweed handed it to her.

'This will be destroyed!' cried Bubblepot, and threw the book on to the fire. It sizzled and hissed in an evil blue flame, and was gone.

'Now your wicked power is at an end, Slimy-weed! But we shall never forget what you did! Go away from Thistleberry and never, never come back!'

Without a word, Slimyweed got on her broomstick and flew away.

'Thank goodness!' shouted Bubblepot. 'Now at last we can have tea!'

The stew was served and everyone agreed that it was the best they had ever tasted. Amelia and the dragon enjoyed it very much, even though it was full of witchy things.

Bubblepot was delighted that her birthday had turned out so well after all. She only hoped that they would never see Slimyweed again. And they never did.